MARSEILLE TRAVEL GUIDE 2024

Your Must-Have Tour Companion To France's Brilliant Mediterranean Treasure

Rita R. Nowlin

TABLE OF CONTENT

CHAPTER 1: INTRODUCTION

Louise had always wanted to visit Marseille, a busy port city located on France's Mediterranean coast. As she stepped off the train and onto the platform, she felt a surge of adrenaline flow through her veins. The salty wind touched her cheeks, bringing the promise of adventure and discovery.

Louise walked through the crowded streets with her trusty rucksack slung over her shoulder, her eyes wide with awe at the kaleidoscope of colours and sounds that surrounded her. The rhythmic conversation of residents blended with the beautiful notes of street musicians to form a symphony that resonated through the cobblestone pathways.

Her first trip was to the famous Vieux Port, the epicentre of Marseille's nautical tradition. As she walked along the quay, she marvelled at the variety of fishing boats floating gently in the harbour, their hulls painted in vivid colours that complemented the turquoise sky above. The aroma of freshly caught fish floated through the air, tantalising her taste buds and whetting her hunger for gastronomic adventure.

With each passing minute, Louise fell further in love with Marseille - its rich history, diversified culture, and undeniable joie de vivre. From the busy marketplaces of Le Panier to the towering heights of Notre-Dame de la Garde, she immersed herself in every aspect of the city, cherishing each moment as if it were a priceless pearl.

As the sun began to set below the horizon, throwing a golden light over the cityscape, Louise found herself on the sands of Prado Beach, admiring the waves as they danced gently on the sand. With the sea wind caressing her skin and the distant laughter of children playing in the surf, she realised that her trip had only just begun.

With a happy grin, Louise muttered a secret thank you to Marseille, pledging to return one day to continue her love affair with this wonderful seaside city.

Facts About Marseille

Marseille has a rich history extending back more than 2,600 years, making it one of France's oldest cities. It was created by Greek immigrants in 600 BC and was originally called Massalia.

Marseille has been a cultural melting pot throughout its history, inspired by Greeks, Romans, Arabs, and many more. This cultural diversity is evident in the architecture, food, and manner of life.

The Vieux-Port (Old Port) is Marseille's heart, where fisherman still sells their daily catch against a backdrop of colourful boats and busy eateries. It's a hive of activity and an ideal location for people-watching.

The majestic Basilique Notre-Dame de la Garde, perched on a hill overlooking the city, is an iconic emblem of Marseille.

Its breathtaking Byzantine-style architecture and panoramic vistas draw people from all over the world.

Marseille is a city that combines historical traditions with contemporary tendencies. Its diversified population helps to create a dynamic atmosphere, with bustling markets, exciting festivals, and a strong cultural scene.

Marseille is a cultural hub with various museums, galleries, and theatres that showcase the city's rich creative legacy. Every cultural aficionado may find something to enjoy, from modern art exhibitions to traditional Provençal folk performances.

Marseille, Provence's main city, provides a gateway to the region's stunning landscapes, quaint towns, and well-known wineries. Visitors may visit the magnificent Calanques National Park or sample local wine and cuisine

Marseille soap, known for its quality and purity, has been made in the city for generations. It is valued for its gentle washing effects and traditional workmanship, as well as its use of natural ingredients like olive oil and sea salt.

Marseille is enthusiastic about football, with Olympique de Marseille (OM) being one of France's most successful and well-supported teams. The Stade Vélodrome is the centre of football excitement, with supporters gathering to cheer on their favourite club.

The city's beautiful surroundings and energetic culture have drawn filmmakers from all over the world. Marseille has served as the setting for several films and television series, adding to its charm and mystery.

History And Geography

History

Marseille is one of France's oldest cities, with a history dating back 2,600 years. Around 600 BC, the Greeks constructed a trade centre known as "Massalia" on the Mediterranean Sea's coasts. The city swiftly grew into a commercial and cultural hub, providing a link between European and Near Eastern cultures.

Marseille has been influenced by several civilizations over the years, including Greek, Roman, Byzantine, and Moorish. It was a key port and military station for the Roman Empire. Over the centuries, Marseille saw periods of prosperity, conquest, and collapse, as well as the horrors of war, pestilence, and political instability.

During the Middle Ages, Marseille became a major maritime trading hub in the Mediterranean, attracting merchants from all across Europe and the Middle East. The city's fortunes fluctuated as it dealt with opposing power disputes and illness outbreaks. Marseille saw industrialization and urban development in the nineteenth century, becoming a significant centre for shipping, industry, and immigration.

Marseille has grown into a thriving metropolis noted for its cultural richness, Mediterranean lifestyle, and active arts scene. It remains a vital economic and cultural hub, attracting people from all over the world to its ancient sites, lively marketplaces, and scenic shoreline.

Geography

Marseille is located on the southern coast of France and overlooks the Gulf of Lion in the Mediterranean Sea. The city is located between the rocky limestone hills of Calanques National Park to the south and the lush plains of Provence to the north.

Marseille's topography is distinguished by its breathtaking natural beauty and diverse landscape. The Calanques, a series of stunning limestone cliffs and fjord-like bays, provide a striking backdrop to the urban, providing possibilities for hiking, rock climbing, and water sports. To the east, the mountainous mountains give way to sandy beaches and isolated bays, creating an idyllic location for leisure and pleasure.

Inland, Marseille is surrounded by rolling hills, vineyards, and olive groves that produce some of France's best wine and olive oil. The city's closeness to the Mediterranean Sea has created its climate, which is hot and dry in the summer and moderate and moist in the winter, making it a great destination for outdoor activities all year.

Culture And Language

Marseille's language shows its multiculturalism. While French is the official language, Marseille is noted for its unique regional dialect, "Marseille-Provence," which combines French, Occitan, Italian, and Arabic characteristics. This language fusion reflects the city's diverse history, moulded by centuries of trade, migration, and cultural interchange.

Marseille's robust arts scene reflects the city's cultural tapestry. The city's Mediterranean appeal has long inspired painters, authors, and filmmakers, with stunning scenery and vibrant neighbourhoods acting as creative backgrounds. Marseille's streets, from the busy Old Port to the ancient Le Panier area, are filled with the sights and sounds of local artists, musicians, and entertainers.

The cuisine is another important aspect of Marseille's culture, with its renowned culinary scene deriving influence from Mediterranean flavours and spices. Marseille's cuisine combines classic Provençal dishes like bouillabaisse and ratatouille with North African specialities like couscous and tagine, creating a tantalising combination of flavours and influences.

Aside from its language and food, Marseille's cultural identity is firmly ingrained in its many groups and customs. The city's eclectic mix is mirrored in its festivals, religious festivities, and traditions, which all combine to form a vivid tapestry of cultural expression.

CHAPTER 2: PLANNING YOUR TRIP

The Best Time To Visit

Spring (March-May): Spring is a wonderful season to visit Marseille. The weather is moderate, with temperatures ranging from pleasant to warm. The city is bursting with flowers, and outdoor activities like trekking in the Calanques or seeing the city's ancient neighbourhoods are delightful without the scorching heat of summer.

Summer (June to August) is the busiest tourism season in Marseille. The weather is bright and sunny, ideal for going to the beach or relaxing at a seaside café. However, keep in mind that major tourist spots might get crowded, and lodging may be more expensive. If you can endure the heat and congestion, summer provides a lively environment with a variety of festivals and events.

Autumn (September-November) is another fantastic season to visit Marseille. The weather continues to warm in September, gradually dropping off as the season advances.

Summer crowds thin away, giving it an ideal time to visit the city's cultural attractions, including museums and galleries. You could even catch some grape harvest festivities in the local wine areas.

Winter (December to February): This is the quietest period to visit Marseille. Temperatures are colder, but seldom fall below freezing, making it an appealing location for winter visitors looking for a warmer environment. Winter is an excellent time to see Marseille's culinary scene, relax in cafés, and visit indoor sites such as the Museum of European and Mediterranean Civilizations (MuCEM).

Visa Requirements

Citizens From The Schengen Area:

No visa is required. If you are a citizen of an EU nation, Iceland, Liechtenstein, Norway, Switzerland, or Andorra, you are allowed to visit Marseille for up to 90 days without a visa. Simply make sure your passport is valid for the duration of your visit.

Citizens From Visa-Exempt Countries:

Short-stay visa waiver: Citizens of numerous other countries, including the United States, Canada, Australia, New Zealand, and Japan, can visit Marseille for up to 90 days in 180 days without a visa. The official French government website (https://france-visas.gouv.fr/en/visa-application-guidelines) has a comprehensive list of visa-exempt nations.

Citizens From Different Countries:

A Schengen visa is necessary. If you are not a citizen of the EU, Iceland, Liechtenstein, Norway, Switzerland, Andorra, or a visa-exempt nation, you will typically require a Schengen visa to visit Marseille. This visa permits you to freely travel inside the Schengen Area, which includes 26 European countries.

Types of Schengen visas:

A short-stay visa (Schengen visa) is valid for up to 90 days within 180 days. Suitable for leisure travel, business excursions, visits to friends and family, and so on.

Long-stay visas are valid for stays of more than 90 days. Required for studying, working, or staying in France for a lengthy duration.

Budgeting Tip

- Consider alternatives to hotels: There are several hostels, guesthouses, and Airbnbs in Marseille that provide economical lodging. If you're travelling with a group, renting an apartment might be a cost-effective solution.

- Book ahead of time: Because Marseille is a popular tourist destination, you should book your accommodations ahead of time, especially if you're visiting during the high season. This will allow you to obtain the best pricing and avoid losing out on availability.

- Staying outside the city centre allows you to locate cheaper lodging choices. Marseille has a decent public transit system, making it simple to travel about.

Transportation:

- Use public transport: The Marseille Metro is a clean, quick, and reasonably priced means to get around the city. You may buy individual tickets or multi-day passes.

- Marseille is a tiny city, so you can easily get around on foot or by bike. This is an excellent way to explore the city while saving money on transportation.

- Avoid taxis: Taxis in Marseille are pricey, so you should avoid them unless necessary.
- Cook your meals: If you live in a flat with a kitchen, preparing your meals is a terrific method to save money on groceries. You may purchase goods at local markets or supermarkets.
- Eat at cafes and restaurants outside of the tourist zones: Cafes and restaurants in tourist regions are often more costly. Venturing outside of the city centre allows you to locate cheaper and more genuine restaurants.
- Try street food: Marseille offers an excellent range of street food, which is a wonderful and inexpensive way to sample local cuisine.
- Have picnics. Pack a picnic lunch and eat it in one of Marseille's numerous parks or gardens. This is an excellent way to save money while enjoying the outdoors.

Activities:

- Take advantage of free activities: There are several free things to see and do in Marseille, like visiting the Notre-Dame de la Garde church, strolling along the Corniche, and exploring the Panier region.

- Look for discounts: Many museums and attractions provide discounts to students, retirees, and families. You may also get bargain passes that provide you access to various attractions.
- Visit during the off-season: If your vacation dates are flexible, try visiting Marseille between October and May. Prices for lodging, transportation, and activities are often reduced during this period.

Getting to Marseille

Arriving By Aeroplane:

Marseille Provence Airport (MRS) is Marseille's major airport, located around 25 km northwest of the city centre.

By Bus: The most affordable method is the Navette Aéroport shuttle bus (line 91), which departs every 20 minutes and takes around 30 minutes to reach Saint-Charles train station or the Silo neighbourhood in the city centre. The fare is about €9.

By Train: Take the free shuttle bus from the airport to Vitrolles-Aéroport train station, then transfer to a TER regional train to Saint-Charles station in the city centre. This travel takes around 45 minutes and costs around €10.

Taxis are widely accessible at the airport, with fixed fares ranging from €50 to €60 to the city centre depending on the time of day. This is a good alternative for small parties or those travelling with heavy luggage.

Arrive Via Train:

Saint-Charles Rail Station: This is Marseille's principal rail station, located in the centre of the city. If you are arriving from other French cities or neighbouring countries such as Italy and Spain, you will most likely disembark here.

By Tram or Metro: The Marseille metro and tram systems are vast and well-connected to the rail station. You may simply purchase tickets from machines at the station and travel to most sections of the city in minutes.

Taxis are available outside the station, giving trips to various sections of the city for metered fees.

Arriving Via Cruise Ship:

Grand Port Maritime de Marseille Fos: Cruise ships land at Gate 4 of this port, which is approximately 6 kilometres from the city centre.

On ship arrival/departure days, a free shuttle service runs from 9 a.m. to 5 p.m., transporting guests to the La Joliette sector in the city centre.

By Bus: Public buses (lines 35T or 35) run regularly from the port to La Joliette, taking around 20 minutes and costing €2.

Taxis are a practical choice, with rates to the city centre starting at €20.

Tips:

If you expect to use public transit frequently during your visit, consider obtaining a Marseille City Pass. It provides unlimited bus, tram, and metro rides, as well as free admission to various museums and attractions.

Download the RTM Marseille app to plan your public transport trips and view live schedules.

Getting Around Marseille

Walking: The greatest way to see Marseille's ambience and hidden jewels is on foot. The ancient Panier neighbourhood and the gorgeous Vieux Port (Old Port) are particularly enjoyable to visit on foot. Also, walking is entirely free!

Public Transportation: Marseille's excellent public transportation network serves the whole city, making it a handy and economical option. Here's an overview of the many alternatives.

- **Metro**: With two lines linking key sites, the metro is quick and simple to use. A single ticket costs €1.70, while a rechargeable Pass Navigo provides unlimited travel for 24 hours (€5.70), 48 hours (€8.80), or 72 hours (€12.30).

- **Trams** offer a pleasant way to explore the city with three lines serving various neighbourhoods. The ticket charges are the same as the metro.

- **Bus**: Marseille's vast bus network connects all parts of the city, making it excellent for longer excursions or getting to the suburbs. Tickets cost €1.70, however a Marseille City Pass provides unlimited use of all public transit for 24, 48, or 72 hours, as well as free admission to museums and attractions. Prices start at €22.

- **Taxis**: Taxis are widely accessible, but metered fees may rapidly add up. Consider ride-sharing applications such as Uber for potentially lower prices.

- **A boat** journey provides a unique perspective of Marseille and its coastline. Prices vary according to the route but expect to spend between €5 and €8 for a one-way ticket.

- **Vélo Bleu, Marseille's bike-sharing programme**, allows you to explore the city at your leisure. Rentals are €1 per day, with savings for longer durations.
- **Car Rental**: Renting a car provides complete flexibility, although Marseille may be difficult to navigate by automobile, especially with few parking alternatives. Consider this choice only if you intend to go beyond the city centre.

Accommodation Options

InterContinental Marseille - Le Grand Hotel Dieu: This ancient hotel has breathtaking views of the Vieux Port and provides luxury accommodations, a Michelin-starred restaurant, and a rooftop pool. Expect to pay more than €500. *Tel: +33 4 91 15 20 00.*

Sofitel Marseille Vieux Port: This hotel, located on the waterfront, features exquisite rooms, a spa, and a rooftop terrace with panoramic views. Rates start at roughly €400 per night. *www.sofitel-marseille-vieuxport.com. Tel: +33 4 91 13 23 23.*

Boutique Hotels

OKKO Hotels Marseille Prado: This contemporary hotel features modern rooms, a rooftop bar with city views, and a co-working area. Prices start at roughly €150 per night. *Tel: +33 4 84 25 83 83.*

Hotel Maison Montgrand: This quaint hotel in the Panier area has distinctive, independently furnished rooms as well as a gorgeous courtyard. Rates start at roughly €100 per night. *Tel: +33 4 91 91 46 46.*

Budget-Friendly Options

Hotel Ibis Marseille Centre Prado: This centrally situated hotel provides simple but pleasant rooms for a reasonable price (about €70 per night). *Tel: +33 4 91 72 90 00*

Hostel Marseille Prado: This vibrant hostel has dorm beds and private rooms, a community kitchen, and a rooftop patio. Prices start at €20 per night. *Tel: +33 4 91 42 29 00*

Vacation Rentals

Consider renting a flat or studio through services such as Airbnb or Booking.com for a more homely atmosphere and the freedom to cook your meals. Prices vary according to location, size, and amenities.

CHAPTER 3: TOP ATTRACTIONS IN MARSEILLE

Vieux Port (Old Port)

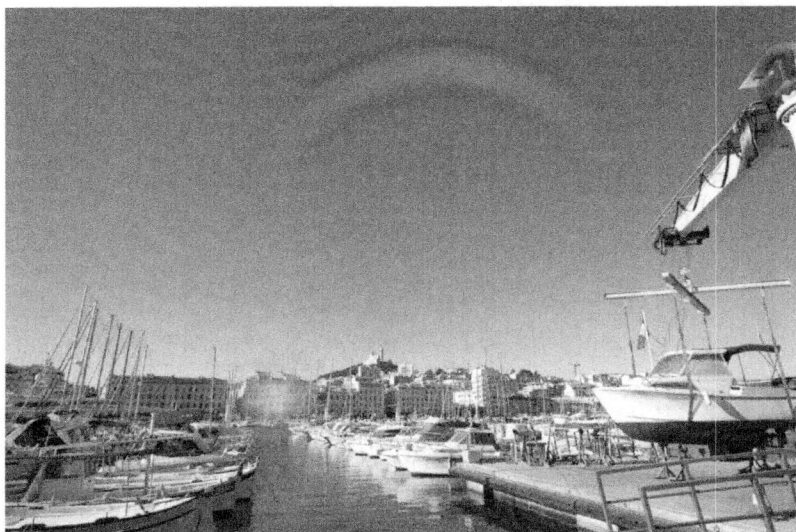

If you're taking public transit, the nearest metro stop is Vieux-Port - Hôtel de Ville (Line 1), which will drop you off right at the port's door. Alternatively, if you're touring the city on foot, simply follow the signs pointing towards the harbour, and you'll soon be immersed in the bustling atmosphere of Vieux Port.

Savour the wealth of the sea by beginning your day in the Quai des Belges, where fisherman proudly show their fresh catch. Snag a booth at a beachfront cafe and enjoy exquisite seafood meals while admiring the bobbing boats. Don't miss out on trying bouillabaisse, Marseille's hallmark meal, which is a flavorful fish stew.

Explore the cultural melting pot by strolling through the lively Marché du Cours Julien, a treasure trove of local goods, spices, and street cuisine. Mix with friendly merchants, take in the bright ambiance, and purchase one-of-a-kind mementos to remember your trip by.

Immerse yourself in Marseille's art scene by visiting the Musée des Civilisations Européennes et Méditerranéennes (MuCEM). This beautiful museum displays the Mediterranean's cultural fabric, fro ancient artefacts to modern exhibits.

Gem:

- Fort Saint-Jean: Escape the throng and visit this mediaeval fort, which provides panoramic views of the city and harbour. Explore the ramparts, learn about the military history, and relax in the gardens.

- Le Panier: Explore the twisting lanes of this ancient area, which was once a sanctuary for sailors and artists. Discover lovely cafés, secluded squares, and colourful facades adorned with street art.
- L'Estaque: Take a boat to this picturesque fishing hamlet for a peaceful getaway. Stroll along the pebble beach, eat fresh seafood at a waterfront restaurant, and take in the stunning Mediterranean views.

Notre-Dame De La Garde

Tel:+33 4 91 13 40 80, www.notredamedelagarde.com/. If you're taking public transportation, buses and taxis often shuttle people to the basilica from various locations across

the city. Alternatively, you may take a leisurely walk or walk up the hill, taking in the beauty as you go.

The Basilica of Notre-Dame de la Garde, commonly known as la Bonne Mère, is a Roman Catholic basilica built atop Marseille's tallest hill.

Skip the tourist train and instead take the concealed 120-step stairway that weaves its way up the hill, providing fascinating local interactions along the way.

Marseille's Heartbeat Attending a service or gospel performance in the basilica will immerse you in the local spirit. Witness the community's strong religious and cultural heritage.

Panier neighbourhood: After your visit, go around the bustling Panier neighbourhood, a maze of little alleys packed with colourful residences, charming cafés, and artisan stores. Savour Marseille's distinctive flavours at a local restaurant or drink a pastis on a sunny balcony.

The Museum of Mediterranean Archaeology, housed within the basilica, boasts an extraordinary collection of artefacts that depict the narrative of Marseille's rich maritime history and cultural legacy.

Gem:

- Vaisseau Mérindol: This former wine warehouse has been turned into a compelling cultural hub that hosts art exhibitions, concerts, and seminars.
- Le Cours Julien: This stylish quarter is recognised for its street art, independent stores, and bustling bars, providing a look into Marseille's alternative lifestyle.

Here are some beauties surrounding Notre Dame de la Garde:

- The Jardins de la Madonne are a magnificent public garden adjacent to the church. They provide wonderful views of the city and are ideal for relaxing and enjoying peace and quiet.
- Vallon des Auffes is a lovely fishing town at the foot of a hill. It's a terrific area to explore and take up the vibe.

- The Corniche Kennedy is a picturesque beachfront route with spectacular views of the Mediterranean Sea. It's an excellent spot to drive or bike.

Tip:

Consider getting a Marseille City Pass for cheaper admission to the Notre-Dame de la Garde and other sites.

Le Panier (Old Town)

www.lepanierdemarseille.com/. Le Panier is situated in the heart of Marseille, near the Old Port. You can easily reach there by walking, bus, or subway.

Le Panier is Marseille's oldest area, known for its steep streets and houses. It's a beautiful, village-like neighbourhood noted for its artistic atmosphere, cool hidden squares, and sun-baked cafes. It's a terrific area to roam about, get lost in the little alleyways, and soak up the local vibe.

Local insights:

- The streets of Le Panier are tiny and twisting, so walking is the ideal way to explore them. Make sure you wear comfy shoes!
- There are many hidden jewels to discover in Le Panier, so don't be afraid to venture off the usual route.
- Try some of the local dishes, such as bouillabaisse (fish stew) or navettes (orange-flavored biscuits).
- Le Panier is an excellent spot to purchase mementos including soap, olive oil, and ceramics.

Gems:

- The Vieille Charité is a 17th-century almshouse that today houses two museums, the Musée d'Archéologie de Marseille and the Musée d'Art Contemporain.
- The Maison Diamantée is a stunning 16th-century home with a distinctive diamond-shaped exterior.
- The Cours Julien is a bustling plaza surrounded by bars, cafés, and restaurants.

- The Marché de la Noailles is a lively market that sells everything from fresh fruit to souvenirs.
- Passage Emeriau: A secret passage leading to a hidden square with charming cafes

Calanques National Park

www.calanques-parcnational.fr/en/, Tel: +33 (4) 42 84 84 84, +33 (4) 42 84 82 20. The Calanques National Park spans the coast between Marseille and Cassis. You may reach there via vehicle, bus, or boat. Public transit is widely available, particularly during the high season.

Consider this: the sun warming your skin as you walk down sun-soaked pathways, the rhythmic crash of waves on the coast, and the enticing aroma of pine and sea air filling your lungs. This is the sensory playground in the Calanques.

Tips:

- Embrace the Calanque spirit by staying on approved pathways and not littering. Remember that you are a visitor in this natural beauty.
- Be sun-savvy. Pack sunscreen, a hat, and sunglasses because the Mediterranean sun may be fierce.
- Shoes with traction: The ground might be rough and uneven, therefore sturdy shoes are required.
- Bring a snorkel: The undersea realm is alive with colourful fish and marine life.
- Explore beyond the crowds: Some calanques are easy to reach, while others demand more effort. Hidden jewels are often found off the usual road, providing you with peace and spectacular vistas.

Gems:

- Calanque de Sugiton: This postcard-perfect cove has crystal-clear seas and a lovely gravel beach. Hike down from the Col de la Gardiole to enjoy breathtaking panoramic views.

- Calanque d'En-Vau: This remote bay, accessible only by boat or a strenuous climb, provides a sense of isolation and unsurpassed natural splendour.
- Méjean Calanque is a refuge for kayakers and snorkelers, with towering cliffs, grottoes, and underwater arches.
- Cosquer Cave: Take a guided trip to see prehistoric cave drawings stretching back 37,000 years. This buried jewel provides insight into Marseille's historical past.

Château D'If

www.chateau-if.fr/ Tel: +33 4 91 19 71 00

The Château is accessible via boat from Marseille's Vieux Port. The trek takes around 20 minutes and provides breathtaking views of the city and beach.

Château d'If, a fortification and prison, was originally built in the 16th century to protect the entrance to Marseille's harbour. However, its most memorable chapter was as a jail, housing notable characters like as Mirabeau and Edmond Dantès, the fictitious hero of Alexandre Dumas' "The Count of Monte Cristo."

For decades, filmmakers have been drawn to the Château because of its dramatic setting and historical attraction. It has served as a setting for a number of films,

Local Insights And Hidden Gems:

- Beyond the Walls: While the Château is the major attraction, the island of If has more to offer. Hike along the picturesque pathways, take in the panoramic views of Marseille, and discover the abandoned Frioul Islands nearby.

- Dive into History: The Château's museum depicts its rich history with displays on its military and prison responsibilities. Discover stories about renowned convicts, escape attempts, and the brutal reality of prison life.

- Secret Corners: Look for secret features engraved into the fortress walls, such as graffiti left by captives wishing for release. Seek find the solitary confinement cell, a vivid reminder of the Château's grim history.

Cathedrale De La Major

+33 4 91 90 71 00 www.*diocese-marseille.fr/paroisse/sanctuaire-sainte-marie-majeure-cathedrale-la-major/*

Take your time admiring the facade's rich elements, such as the sculptures, mosaics, and stained glass windows. Don't forget to go around the church and observe it from different perspectives.

The cathedral's interior is equally stunning as its appearance, with soaring ceilings, colourful mosaics, and intricate ornaments. Be sure to see the main altar, the crypt, and the treasury.

The church is built on a hilltop and provides breathtaking views over the Old Port and Marseille. Take some time to enjoy the scenery and the fresh air.

If you're lucky enough to be in Marseille on a Sunday, you may attend a mass in the cathedral and feel the spiritual energy of this hallowed site.

Local Insights:
- Better time to visit: The cathedral is open all year, however it's better to avoid peak visitor hours, which are usually in the afternoon. If you want to avoid crowds, go early in the morning or late in the day.
- Dress code: There is no official dress requirement, although it is encouraged that you dress modestly to respect the religious essence of the area.

- The cathedral is accessible to those with impairments. The cathedral has a ramp leading up to the entrance, as well as lifts inside.
- Guided tours of the cathedral are offered in both English and French. These tours provide an excellent opportunity to learn more about the cathedral's history and architecture.

Gems:

- The cathedral's crypt, located under the main altar, includes the remains of notable historical individuals from Marseille. It's a fantastic site to visit and learn about the city's history.
- The treasury of the cathedral has a collection of sacred artefacts such as gold and silver tableware, jewellery, and vestments. It is a tiny yet intriguing collection that provides insight into the church's richness and history.
- The rooftop terrace of the cathedral provides even more breathtaking views of the city than the ground level. It's an excellent area to unwind and take in the view. However, access to the rooftop terrace is temporarily blocked due to renovations.

Vallon Des Auffes

It is located at a short distance from Marseille's city centre and can be reached by vehicle, public transit, or even on foot if you want to take a lovely stroll along the shore.

Vallon des Auffes is a tiny fishing harbour famous for its brightly coloured buildings, traditional fishing boats, and seafood restaurants. The location is also a popular swimming and sunbathing destination.

As you walk through the small alleyways surrounded with colourful fishermen's huts, you'll feel the history and character of this area permeate your spirit. The charming harbour, studded with traditional fishing boats, looks lovely against the azure seas of the Mediterranean Sea.

Vallon des Auffes offers several local perspectives. Start a discussion with the friendly fishermen and townspeople, and you'll learn stories passed down through generations. They could provide recommendations for the finest places to eat fresh seafood or the most gorgeous walking pathways along the shore.

There are hidden jewels around every turn. There are plenty of hidden gems to discover, from tucked-away seafood eateries serving up the catch of the day to lovely cafés with panoramic views of the sea.

Local Insights and Gem:

- Visit the fish market: The fish market in Vallon des Auffes is an excellent place to get fresh seafood directly from local fisherman. Other produce options include fruits, veggies, and cheese.
- Take a boat tour: Several businesses provide boat tours of the Vallon des Auffes and the adjacent shoreline. This

is an excellent method to gain a new perspective on the place while also learning about its history.

- Take a walk: There are various hiking routes in the neighbourhood that provide breathtaking views of the Vallon des Auffes and the Mediterranean Sea. The most popular walk is the Sentier des douaniers, which runs along the cliffs above the harbour.

- Picnic on the beach: A little beach near the Vallon des Auffes is ideal for a picnic meal. There are no restaurants or shops nearby, so bring your own food and beverages.

- Attend a local festival: The Vallon des Auffes has several festivals and events throughout the year. These are an excellent opportunity to learn about the local culture and meet some of the people that live there.

Here are some highly recommended eateries in the area:

- Chez Fonfon: This long-running restaurant is famous for its bouillabaisse soup and Mediterranean fish dishes. *www.chez-fonfon.com/, Tel: +33 4 91 52 14 38*

- L'Avant Cour serves a tasting menu that changes seasonally. *www.lavant-cour-restaurant-marseille.com/, Tel: +33 4 91 25 04 84*

- L'Épuisette: This exquisite waterfront restaurant serves seafood-focused fixed-price meals and has a comprehensive wine selection. *www.l-epuisette.fr/*, *Tel: +33 4 91 52 17 82*

- Chez Jeannot: Enjoy pizzas and grilled foods while seeing the sunset. *www.pizzeriachezjeannot.com/*
- Viaghiji Di Fonfon: This seafood restaurant belongs to the Chez Fonfon company. *www.viaghjidifonfon.com/en/*

Abbaye Saint Victor

www.saint-victor.net/, *Tel: +33 4 91 52 81 00. Take the metro to the "Cours Julien" station or bus 54, 55, or 60 to the "Place Saint Victor" stop.*

Admire the spectacular Romanesque architecture, including the nave, apse, and cloister. Look for beautiful sculptures and colourful mosaics on the walls.

Descend to the crypt, where the abbey's founders and other notable persons are interred. The ambiance is both creepy and interesting, with sarcophagi and bones decorating the walls.

Enjoy a tranquil time at the abbey's serene grounds, which provide a welcome break from the city's hustle and bustle. Climb the bell tower for stunning panoramic views of Marseille and the surrounding region (260 steps).

The Abbaye Saint Victor is situated in the Panier area, Marseille's oldest neighbourhood. Before or after seeing the abbey, explore its small alleys, lovely squares, and local shops.

The abbey occasionally organises concerts, exhibits, and other activities. Visit their website for additional details.

There are several cafés and restaurants in the Panier neighbourhood where you may sample delectable Provençal fare.

Gems:

- The Romanesque crypt: While the main crypt is highly renowned, there is a smaller, secret Romanesque crypt under the cathedral that few people visit. If you want to explore this hidden gem, ask the staff for access.
- The abbey's library: The monastery has a collection of historic manuscripts and volumes that are not open to the public, although visitors may enjoy the gorgeous library hall from the outside.
- The view from the Fort Saint-Jean: Situated immediately next to the abbey, the Fort Saint-Jean provides breathtaking views of Marseille harbour and the Mediterranean Sea.

Orange Velodrome

www.orangevelodrome.com/, Tel: +33 4 91 72 22 22.The stadium is located in the city's south and is easily accessible either metro (Line 2) or tram (Line 3).

The Orange Vélodrome is a multipurpose stadium and is located in Marseille's Euroméditerranée sector, which has undergone redevelopment. There are several cafés, restaurants, and stores in the vicinity, as well as a museum dedicated to the history of the Orange Vélodrome.

If you want to discover more about the Orange Vélodrome's history, take a guided tour of the stadium. Tours are accessible in both French and English.

Watch the famed Olympique de Marseille (OM) team electrify the enthusiastic audience. The chanting, the pyrotechnics, the energy--it's an incredible experience!

The Velodrome isn't only for football. Catch concerts, rugby tournaments, or even cultural events to take up the eclectic vibe.

Indulge in the local cuisine scene around the stadium. From fresh seafood to substantial stews, satisfy your cravings before or after the game.

Gems:

- The OM Museum explores the club's rich history, championships, and iconic players. Interactive exhibitions let the stories come to life.
- The Presidential Box: For a taste of VIP luxury, plan a visit to the Presidential Box, which offers breathtaking panoramic views of the pitch and city.

- The Roof: Take a guided visit to the stadium's roof for stunning city views and a unique perspective.
- There are several parks and gardens around the Orange Vélodrome, including the Parc Borely and the Jardin du Pharo. These are excellent spots to unwind and enjoy the outdoors.

Museums And Cultural Institutions

MuCEM (Museum of European and Mediterranean Civilisations)

www.mucem.org/ MuCEM, with its remarkable contemporary building built by Rudy Ricciotti and Roland Carta, is more than just a museum; it represents the fusion of tradition and modernity. The elegant facade of latticed concrete pays respect to the region's architectural tradition while also representing openness and connectedness.

Step into MuCEM and you'll be immersed in a voyage through the various civilizations that formed Europe and the Mediterranean. MuCEM's shows range from ancient artefacts to modern art installations, providing a comprehensive investigation of history, culture, and identity.

One of MuCEM's most notable aspects is its commitment to promoting communication and understanding among diverse cultures and peoples. MuCEM acts as a cultural exchange and learning hub with its dynamic programme of events, lectures, and workshops.

During your visit, be sure to check out the museum's panoramic terrace, which provides stunning views of Marseille's historic Old Port and the glittering Mediterranean beyond. It's an ideal location to ponder on the vast tapestry of human experience that MuCEM so wonderfully captures.

Palais Longchamp

www.marseille.fr/palais-longchamp, Tel:+33 4 91 55 25 25.
Palais Longchamp is conveniently accessible by public
transit and is a must-see attraction for both visitors and
residents.

You'll discover thorough information on current exhibitions,
their historical relevance, and practical details like ticket
costs and guided tour schedules.

Palais Longchamp, with its towering architecture and eclectic
collection of art and artefacts, offers an unforgettable trip
through Marseille's cultural tapestry. Whether you're a

history buff, an art lover, or simply inquisitive about the city's history, a visit to Palais Longchamp will make an indelible impact.

Musée Des Beaux-Arts

Imagine walking through hallways filled with masterpieces from centuries of artistic expression. From Renaissance masterpieces to modern wonders, the Musée des Beaux-Arts has a broad collection that never fails to attract visitors.

As you go through the museum's galleries, you'll come across pieces by great painters like Van Gogh, Picasso, and Monet, each with its own distinct narrative and enticing you to immerse yourself in its beauty.

But the Musée des Beaux-Arts is more than simply a collection of paintings; it's a window into Marseille's rich cultural history. The museum's exhibitions and educational programmes commemorate the city's robust creative legacy while also providing visitors with a greater knowledge of its past and present.

Those planning a visit may readily locate the Musée des Beaux-Arts in Marseille's Palais Longchamp area. To avoid missing out on any forthcoming exhibitions or activities, visit their website at *www.musee-des-beaux-arts-marseille.com*. Additionally, you may call them at *+33 (0)4 91 14 59 00*.

CHAPTER 4: DINING AND CUISINE

Local Specialties

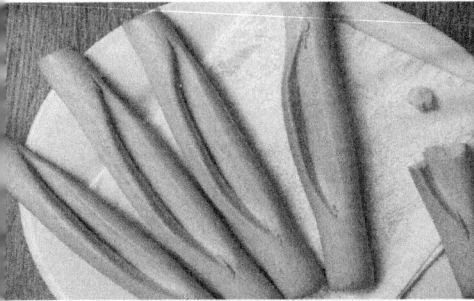

Imagine yourself strolling through the busy streets, guided by the seductive aroma of freshly made pastries emanating from the corner bakery. Marseille is famous for its wonderful pastries, including the distinctive Navettes—a sweet, boat-shaped cookie flavoured with orange blossom water—and the enticing Calissons, almond-shaped confections created with crushed almonds and candied fruit.

But Marseille's culinary delights go far beyond pastries. Prepare to enjoy a symphony of flavours at the city's lively markets, where vendors overflow with fresh seafood straight from the Mediterranean sea. Dive into a plate of Bouillabaisse, Marseille's famous fish stew, filled with a variety of local catch cooked to perfection in a fragrant broth of tomatoes, saffron, and herbs.

Don't forget about the renowned Panisse, a savoury chickpea flour fritter with a crispy exterior and a fluffy, melt-in-your-mouth interior. Pair it with a big dollop of aioli, Marseille's famous garlic-infused mayonnaise, for a gastronomic experience that will leave you wanting more.

While exploring Marseille's culinary scene, don't miss out on sampling the city's renowned street food specialties, such as Socca—a savoury chickpea pancake cooked to crispy perfection in a wood-fired oven—and Pissaladière, a mouthwatering tart topped with caramelised onions, olives, and anchovies.

Marseille's native specialties, which range from the tantalising aroma of freshly caught seafood to the soothing warmth of a typical bouillabaisse, reflect the city's rich culinary legacy and lively cultural tapestry. So, indulge your senses, savour each bite, and let Marseille's flavours take you on a gastronomic journey unlike any other.

Restaurants And Cafés

Au Bord de l'Eau, a local favourite, delivers fresh seafood in a casual environment. It is positioned directly on the waterfront in the Vallon des Auffes area, with breathtaking views of the harbour. Getting there: Take bus #83 from the city centre to Pointe Rouge, then walk for around 10 minutes to the restaurant. *Phone number is +33 4 91 52 45 20.*

L'Épuisette is a Michelin-starred restaurant with a unique touch on French Mediterranean cuisine. The restaurant is located in the Plage de l'Anse de Malmousque neighbourhood, which is famous for its gorgeous beaches. Getting there: Take the #21 bus from Saint-Charles Station to David. The restaurant is only a short walk from there. Reservations can be made through their website, *www.l-epuisette.fr/, or by calling +33 4 91 52 93 81.*

Cafe Simon is a historic cafe in the city centre that is ideal for a relaxing breakfast or lunch break. They serve a variety of coffee beverages, pastries, and savoury foods. Getting there: The cafe is very near to the Bourse metro station, making it quite easy to find. *Their telephone number is +33 4 91 33 05 14.*

La Chimère Café has a modern coffee shop vibe and is ideal for coffee lovers and brunch fans. They serve specialised coffee drinks, handmade pastries and savoury brunch items. The cafe is in the Cours Julien sector, a hip neighbourhood known for its street art and shopping. Getting there: Take the Tram T2 to Cours Julien. The cafe is situated right on the main strip. *Their phone number is +33 4 91 54 95 34.*

Markets And Street Food

The lively *Marché des Capucins*, located in the centre of Marseille, is an iconic market that you must see. Fresh vegetables, fragrant spices, gourmet cheeses, and other items are proudly displayed by merchants amidst the bustling talk of consumers. Take your time exploring the stalls, interacting with merchants, and sampling some of the region's best items.

To get a flavour of Marseille's numerous culinary influences, visit the *Marché de Noailles*, where you'll find an unusual mix of exotic cuisines and spices. From North African specialties to Middle Eastern delights, this market is a melting pot of flavours that represents the city's diverse ethnic background.

As you tour Marseille's streets, be sure to try the city's bustling street food culture. From savoury socca, a well cooked chickpea pancake, to aromatic bouillabaisse, a classic fish stew overflowing with Mediterranean flavours, the city's streets are loaded with delectable treats ready to be enjoyed.

Don't pass up the opportunity to try panisses, a popular local snack made of crispy chickpea fritters, or fresh fish cooked simply and served with a lemon squeeze. Wash it all down with a refreshing glass of pastis, an anise-flavored liqueur that is a staple of Marseille's drinking culture.

Nightlife And Entertainment

Bars And Clubs

The Vintage Club is the place for you. On Thursday through Saturday nights, this vibrant place in the city centre changes into a karaoke bar, complete with a welcoming environment and a diverse song selection. The most convenient method to get there is by using the subway. Bourse is the closest station on the M1 line. From there, head east on Rue Paradis and then south on Rue Glandeves. The*ir telephone number is +33 6 23 65 57 18.*

Baby Club is a Marseille institution known for its electrifying electro and house music nights. With big-name DJs and a powerful sound system, this small club is a terrific location to dance the night away. This club is also close to the Bourse metro station (line M1). From the station, head south on Rue Paradis before turning left onto Rue André Poggioli. Their website is *www.zagip.com/baby-club-marseille/. Their telephone number is +33 6 19 98 29 22.*

N/B: Please be aware that both Le Vintage Club and Baby Club are closed on Mondays, Tuesdays, and Sundays.

Le Bar de la Marine is a favourite hangout for both residents and visitors. It is located in the Vieux Port district and serves a wide variety of beverages and snacks.

Live Music Venues

Dock des Suds, a cultural hub on Marseille's docks, is a well-known venue for its alternative music scene. They frequently offer performances that include Rock, Hip Hop, Electro, and other genres. They also host the yearly Babel Music Experience, an international music event that brings together artists from all over the globe. **Getting There:** Take metro line M2 to Arenc Arenc Metro Station, then walk a short distance. You can also take buses 83 or 85 to the Arenc Le Silo stop.*Website: www.dock-des-suds.org/. Phone Number: +33 (0)4 91 99 00 00.*

If you want a more intimate setting, *Le Moulin* is an excellent option. This intimate venue in the Cours Julien district is well-known for showcasing emerging local and international artists. They primarily feature indie, rock, and alternative genres. **Getting There**: Take the M1 metro line to Cours Julien, which is located next to the station. *Website:*

https://lemoulin.org/marseille/ (only in French). Phone Number: +33 4 91 54 95 89.

L'Espace Julien, another Cours Julien landmark, is a famed music theatre that has served as a springboard for many French performers. They provide a varied range of concerts, including rock, pop, electro, and world music. **Getting Here:** Take metro line M1 to Cours Julien and walk a short distance from the station. *Website: https://www.espace-julien.com/fr/ (in French only). Phone Number: +33 4 91 54 73 33.*

For jazz enthusiasts, *Le Cri du Port* is a must-see. This jazz club in the Panier area has a cosy ambiance and hosts a variety of local and international jazz performers. **Getting There:** Take the M1 metro line to Colbert et Canadian, then walk a short distance. You may also take bus lines 83 or 85 to the Criminal Investigation Department Colbert station. *Website: www.criduport.fr/ (French only). Phone: +33 4 91 50 51 41.*

Le Molotov is the place to be if you enjoy a lively atmosphere and a diverse range of music. This renowned establishment in the Mazarin neighbourhood hosts live music performances ranging from rock and alternative to electro and DJ sets. **Getting There:** Take the M2 metro line to Saint-Charles, then walk about 10 minutes. You can also take bus lines 21, 55, or 83 to the Saint-Charles Trinité stop. *Website: www.facebook.com/LemolotovMarseille. (French Only): +33 6 22 40 04 26.*

Theatres and Performance Spaces

Opéra de Marseille: This renowned opera house presents an enthralling programme of operas, ballets, and recitals. The Opéra de Marseille is famous for its massive architecture and excellent acoustics. **Getting There:**You may easily reach there by taking the metro to the Colbert or Vieux-Port stations. *Their phone number is +33 4 91 54 75 75.*

La Criée - National Theatre of Marseille: This contemporary theatre is a refuge for individuals looking for new and experimental performances. Throughout the year, La Criée hosts a variety of theatrical, dance, and musical acts. **Getting There**: Metro lines M1 and M2 connect to the Colbert station. *www.lacriee.com/ or phone +33 4 91 91 11 21*

Théâtre du Gymnase: This old theatre on Marseille's lively Canebière street is a local institution. The Théâtre du Gymnase, founded in 1787, features a diverse programme of comedies, dramas, and one-man acts. **Getting There**: located on lines M1 and M2, is the closest metro station. For additional information, contact *+33 4 91 91 11 19.*

Théâtre Silvain: If you're looking for an outdoor theatre experience, Théâtre Silvain is the place to go. This theatre, nestled amidst the beautiful foliage of the Vallon de la Fausse-Monnaie, hosts a lovely programme of concerts, plays, and outdoor cinema screenings throughout the summer months.**Getting there**:To get to the theatre, take bus lines 21 or 83. *You may discover their programme on the Marseille Tourism website or phone +33 4 91 14 54 10 for more information.*

Shopping in Marseille

High-End Shopping:

Rue Paradis and Rue Grignan: Dubbed the "Golden Triangle," this exclusive neighbourhood is a magnet for luxury products. Stroll down Rue Paradis and Rue Grignan, and you'll be surrounded by flagship boutiques for renowned brands like as Louis Vuitton, Chanel, Dior, and many more. Expect to be wowed by the stunning window displays and luxury stores.

Centre Bourse: This modern retail mall in the city centre features a diverse selection of stores, including high-end brands like as Maje, Sandro, and Claudie Pierlot. It also has a range of casual clothes stores, beauty shops, and eateries, making it an ideal one-stop shopping destination.

Unique Boutiques And Local Finds:

Le Panier: This ancient quarter is a fascinating maze of little alleyways filled with individual businesses and artisan crafts. Explore the one-of-a-kind businesses that sell local crafts, jewellery, apparel, and home furnishings. You can perhaps upon one-of-a-kind treasures and hidden jewels crafted by skilled local artists.

Cours Julien is known for its bohemian and creative environment, and it is home to independent boutiques, antique stores, and concept stores. Browse the varied variety of apparel, accessories, art, and home décor, all of which represent the merchants' own styles.

Market And Flea Markets:

The Old Port Fish Market: Immerse yourself in the bustling ambiance of the Old Port Fish Market, which runs every morning. Witness the fresh catch of the day exhibited on stalls and learn about local fishermen's lifestyle.

Marché Noailles: This busy market in the city centre is a sensory delight. Explore the maze of stalls filled with fresh vegetables, local specialties, spices, apparel, and other items. Prepare for a lively and exciting shopping experience.

Flea Markets: Marseille has various flea markets, including the Brocante d'Estaque and the Brocante de la Plaine. These treasure troves are ideal for locating unusual vintage things, antiques, furniture, and collectibles at discounted costs.

Tips

- Most establishments are normally open Monday through Saturday, with some extending their hours on Thursday. Malls typically offer extended hours, frequently including Sundays.
- Marseille has two main sales seasons: Soldes d'Hiver (winter sales) in January and February, and Soldes d'Été (summer sales) in July and August. During certain times, you may discover fantastic prices on apparel and other items.
- Most retailers take credit cards, however smaller shops may prefer cash.

CHAPTER 5: DAY TRIPS FROM MARSEILLE

Cassis

Begin your journey in Marseille by taking the short and convenient train from Marseille Saint-Charles station to Cassis. Trains depart routinely, making it simple to organise your journey around your chosen timetable. The ride takes around 25-30 minutes, so you may reach at Cassis quickly and comfortably.

Upon arrival, you will be engulfed in the lovely atmosphere of Cassis. Begin your trip by meandering through the charming streets lined with pastel-colored houses, stores, and welcoming cafés. Take in the Mediterranean beauty as you make your way to the bustling Old Port, where fishing boats sway gently against the backdrop of azure waters.

One of the attractions of a day trip to Cassis is the chance to visit the stunning Calanques. The beautiful limestone cliffs and turquoise coves represent the region's natural beauty. Take a boat excursion or go on a scenic walk to see these geological wonders up close, marvelling at their raw majesty and immaculate surrounds. Don't forget to bring your camera to capture the breathtaking scenery along the journey.

After your Calanques trip, enjoy some relaxing activities and gastronomic pleasures in Cassis. Relax on the sandy beaches of Plage de la Grande Mer, or have a refreshing dip in the crystal-clear waters. Then, treat yourself to a delicious seafood lunch at one of the quaint seaside restaurants, where you can savour the freshest catch of the day combined with local wines like Cassis white wine, which is known for its crisp flavour and fragrant overtones.

As the day comes to a close, enjoy the last minutes of peace in Cassis before returning to Marseille. Catch the train back from Cassis to Marseille, thinking on the remarkable experiences and memories made during your day journey along the magnificent Mediterranean coast.

Aix-en-Provence

There are various suitable routes from Marseille to Aix-en-Provence. Train travel is a popular alternative, with frequent departures from Marseille's Saint-Charles station to Aix-en-Provence's Gare d'Aix-en-Provence. The trek takes around 30-40 minutes and includes lovely views of the countryside along the route.

When you arrive in Aix-en-Provence, you will find yourself surrounded by small cobblestone alleys, magnificent boulevards, and lovely squares. Take a leisurely stroll around the historic district, where you can see wonderfully maintained buildings, local markets, and quaint stores.

Aix-en-Provence is well-known for its cultural history, which includes attractions like the Cours Mirabeau, a tree-lined boulevard lined with cafés and fountains, and the historic Saint-Sauveur Cathedral, a spectacular example of Provençal Romanesque design. Don't miss the opportunity to see the Atelier Cézanne, artist Paul Cézanne's old studio, which provides insight into his life and work.

Savour the gastronomic joys of Provence by trying local delicacies like calissons (almond sweets), classic Provençal cuisine, and pleasant rosé wines. Aix-en-Provence has several cafés, restaurants, and bakeries where you may sample the local cuisine.

Take advantage of Aix-en-Provence's peaceful surroundings by visiting one of its several parks and gardens, such as the Jardin d'Albertas or the Parc Jourdan. Alternatively, you may spend a relaxing afternoon at one of the city's spas or thermal baths, which are known for their medicinal benefits.

After a day of discovery and leisure in Aix-en-Provence, take the return train from Gare d'Aix-en-Provence to Marseille's Saint-Charles station to complete your day trip. To guarantee a smooth return travel to Marseille, check train timetables ahead of time.

Avignon

To begin your day excursion, take a high-speed train from Marseille's Saint-Charles train station to Avignon's main rail station, Gare d'Avignon Centre. The train ride normally takes

30 to 40 minutes, providing a pleasant and quick method to get to your destination.

Alternatively, if you want a more leisurely travel with the freedom to explore the picturesque countryside, you may take a bus or rent a vehicle for the day. The trip from Marseille to Avignon takes around an hour and thirty minutes, and you may enjoy the lovely scenery of Provence along the route.

When you arrive in Avignon, you'll discover a treasure mine of historical landmarks and cultural attractions. Make sure to see the magnificent Palais des Papes, a UNESCO World Heritage Site that functioned as the popes' palace in the 14th century. Wander through the old town's meandering alleyways, where lovely cafés, shops, and art galleries await at every turn.

Don't pass up the opportunity to walk across the Pont d'Avignon, also known as the Pont Saint-Bénézet, a famous mediaeval bridge that crosses the Rhône River and provides beautiful views of the city and surrounding countryside.

If you have time, consider visiting the adjacent Châteauneuf-du-Pape vineyards, where you can participate in wine tastings and savour the flavours of the region's renowned wines.

Before returning to Marseille, have a delightful supper at one of Avignon's typical Provencal restaurants, where you can try local favourites like ratatouille, bouillabaisse, and lavender-flavored sweets.

As the day comes to an end, you may retrace your steps and return to Marseille, savouring the memories of your fascinating day excursion to Avignon and the gems you found along the route.

Arles

Train: One of the most convenient methods to get from Marseille to Arles is via rail. The travel takes around 30-40 minutes and departs often throughout the day from Marseille Saint-Charles rail station.

Car: If you value flexibility and freedom, hiring a car allows you to explore Arles and the surrounding countryside at your leisure. The travel takes around one hour along the A7 highway.

Arles is famous for its well-preserved Roman remains, which include the UNESCO-listed Roman Amphitheatre and

Roman Theatre. As you travel among these antique marvels, you may envision life in Roman Gaul.

Arles is also significant in the art world, notably for Vincent van Gogh, who lived and worked there for a while. Follow along the footsteps of the Dutch maestro by seeing renowned locations such as the Yellow Café (Café Van Gogh) and the Hospital, where he created some of his most famous paintings.

Walk through the tiny alleyways of Arles' old centre, enjoying the mediaeval buildings, lovely squares, and bustling marketplaces. Don't miss the magnificent Saint-Trophime Cathedral and the charming Place de la République.

Arles has various museums that highlight its cultural heritage and creative past. Visit the Fondation Vincent van Gogh Arles to witness exhibitions commemorating the artist's stay in the city, or visit the Musée Réattu, located in a former 15th-century priory and displaying a rich collection of artworks spanning generations.

Arles is globally known for its annual Rencontres d'Arles photographic festival, which takes place throughout the summer months. Even if you don't come during the festival, you may still see photography galleries and exhibitions around town.

Experience the flavours of Provencal food at one of Arles' many restaurants and cafés. Try local dishes like ratatouille, bouillabaisse, and crispy socca, complemented by a glass of delicious rosé wine from the adjacent vineyard.

CHAPTER 6: OUTDOOR ACTIVITIES

Hiking

Calanques National Park: One of Marseille's most famous natural beauties, the Calanques has a plethora of hiking routes that snake through steep limestone cliffs, secret bays, and turquoise seas. Choose from a variety of paths suited to different ability levels, ranging from easy walks along the coast to more difficult routes with steep climbs and descents. Don't miss the opportunity to see panoramic views of the Mediterranean Sea from the summits of Mont Puget and Cap Morgiou.

Montagne Sainte-Victoire: A short drive from Marseille, Montagne Sainte-Victoire entices hikers with its spectacular silhouette and varied terrain. Follow in the footsteps of French painter Paul Cézanne as you explore the mountain's craggy pathways, going through pine woods, olive gardens, and limestone crags. The Grand Baou route provides a satisfying trek to the peak, where you may enjoy panoramic views of the surrounding farmland and distant shoreline.

The Massif de l'Étoile, located near Marseille's city centre, offers several chances for hiking and outdoor activity. Explore its network of pathways snaking through deep Mediterranean scrubland, oak woodlands, and rocky outcrops. The GR 2013 long-distance track is a difficult but rewarding route that encircle the whole massif, highlighting its varied natural beauty and cultural legacy.

Camargue Regional Nature Park: For a change of scenery, head to the Camargue, a large wetland wilderness located west of Marseille. Lace up your hiking boots and explore the calm marshes, salt flats, and coastal dunes, keeping an eye out for native animals like flamingos, wild horses, and black bulls. The Sentier de la Digue à la Mer path is a picturesque walk along the coast that allows you to enjoy panoramic views of the Mediterranean and witness migrating birds in their natural environment.

Tips:
- Wear strong hiking shoes and carry lots of water, sunscreen, and snacks to keep you hydrated and energised during your excursion.

- Check local weather conditions and trail closures before heading out, especially during the summer when temperatures can rise.
- Respect the natural environment and observe the Leave No Trace principles to minimise your influence on vulnerable ecosystems and wildlife habitats.

Water Sports

Kayaking and canoeing: Paddle along Marseille's magnificent coastline to discover secret coves, clean beaches, and towering cliffs from the sea. Whether you're a beginner or an expert paddler, there are guided excursions and rental choices for kayaking and canoeing that will let you to take in the spectacular vistas of Calanques National Park and the Frioul archipelago.

Stand-Up Paddleboarding (SUP): Glide over the Mediterranean's crystal-clear seas on a stand-up paddleboard to get a unique view of Marseille's coastline. SUP is an excellent method to improve balance, build core muscles, and enjoy the tranquil beauty of the water. Rent a paddleboard or take a guided trip to see gorgeous paths and hidden jewels along the shore.

Windsurfing and Kitesurfing: With its constant wind conditions and large beaches, Marseille is a haven for windsurfers and kitesurfers of all ability levels. Feel the thrill of excitement as you use the wind's force to glide across the waves and execute amazing feats. Lessons and equipment rentals are available at several water sports facilities around the coast, making it simple to get started or develop your abilities.

Scuba diving and snorkelling: Explore the Mediterranean's underwater environment, which is rich with marine life, colourful corals, and historic shipwrecks. Whether you're a licenced diver or a novice, dive centres in Marseille provide guided dives, training, and snorkelling trips to discover the Mediterranean Sea's amazing biodiversity.

Sailing and Boat Tours: Set sail on an exciting sailing trip or take a beautiful boat tour to discover Marseille's stunning coastline, quiet harbours, and famous sites from the sea.

Beaches

Prado Beach: Located along Marseille's famed Corniche Kennedy, Prado Beach is a popular area for sunbathing and swimming. Spread your towel on the silky golden sand, soak in the Mediterranean sun, and cool yourself in the blue seas. If you're feeling daring, you may even try your hand at water activities like paddleboarding, windsurfing, and kayaking.

Plage des Catalans, tucked away near the Vieux Port, provides a more intimate environment with its tiny strip of pebbled beach. Despite its tiny size, this beach emanates charm and tranquilly, making it ideal for a relaxing day by the sea. Take a leisurely stroll down the promenade, admiring the views of the Château d'If in the distance, or have a picnic with fresh baguettes and local foods from adjacent markets.

Pointe Rouge Beach: For a family-friendly beach experience, visit Pointe Rouge Beach on Marseille's southern shore. This sandy stretch of shoreline has quiet, shallow seas perfect for swimming and paddling, making it a popular destination for families with children. You may also rent pedal boats or snorkel to explore the vibrant underwater environment.

Calanques National Park: Although not classic beaches, the mountainous shoreline of Calanques National Park provides unrivalled opportunity for outdoor activity. Hike along gorgeous coastal pathways to secret coves and isolated beaches where you may relax in nature and see the magnificent limestone cliffs that plunge into the crystal-clear seas below. Don't forget your camera to capture the stunning scenery along the journey.

Sailing Excursions: Join a sailing adventure to see Marseille's coastline from a new viewpoint. Join a guided boat trip or hire a private sailboat to discover quiet coves, beautiful beaches, and uninhabited islands that are unreachable by land. Whether you're an experienced sailor or a first-time visitor, sailing provides a unique opportunity to admire Marseille's natural beauty and nautical tradition.

CHAPTER 7: PRACTICAL INFORMATION

Language

French is the official language of Marseille, as it is across France. The vast majority of signage, menus, and government correspondence are written in French. Even though many people in Marseille speak English, especially in tourist areas, knowing a few basic French words might be useful.

Marseille's rich linguistic legacy is affected by Occitan, a Romance language spoken in southern France. While Occitan is no longer as commonly spoken as it once was, you may still see remnants of it in local dialects, place names, or cultural references.

Marseille is a cultural melting pot, with large communities of North African, Italian, and Corsican heritage, among others. As a result, you may hear different languages spoken on the streets, including Arabic, Italian, and numerous African languages. This variety contributes to the city's dynamic vibe and unique linguistic tapestry.

Marseille Provencal, sometimes known as Marseillais, is a unique dialect that exists alongside normal French in Marseille. This dialect represents the city's own personality, as seen by its colourful phrases, pronunciation variances, and distinctive vocabulary. While you don't have to speak Marseille Provencal to get by, residents usually appreciate tourists who make an effort to learn about the local culture and language.

No matter what language is spoken, Marseillais are famed for their warmth and welcome. Even if there are language limitations, communicate with a smile, gestures, and simple sentences. Locals like tourists who show an interest in their culture and are typically eager to assist or converse.

Currency

The euro (€) is the official currency of France, including Marseille. Euros are accepted in all transactions, including shopping, dining, transportation, and lodging.

If you need to convert currency, there are currency exchange offices (bureaux de change) all across Marseille, especially in tourist districts, major rail stations, and airports. Furthermore, many banks provide currency exchange services, albeit the prices may differ.

ATMs are extensively available in Marseille and accept all major international credit and debit cards, including Visa, MasterCard, and Maestro. Using ATMs is typically the most convenient option to withdraw Euros, but be aware of any costs paid by your bank for overseas transactions.

Credit cards are frequently accepted throughout Marseille, particularly in hotels, restaurants, stores, and bigger institutions. The most often accepted cards are Visa and MasterCard, followed by American Express and other major credit card brands. However, it is always a good idea to keep some cash on hand for minor transactions or in case you come into a business that does not accept credit cards.

Tipping in Marseille is optional because a service fee is frequently included in the bill at restaurants and cafés. However, it is normal to offer a modest tip (between 5 and 10%) for great service or if you are especially pleased with your experience.

Safety: As with any other city, keep your money and possessions safe while touring Marseille. Use caution when using ATMs, especially in congested places, and consider utilising a money belt or lockable wallet to prevent theft.

Safety Tips

Stay Aware of Your Environment: Marseille is a thriving city with dynamic neighbourhoods and different communities. Maintain vigilance and awareness of your surroundings, particularly in congested tourist destinations, marketplaces, and public transit hubs.

Secure Your Property: Like any major tourist site, Marseille can draw pickpockets and petty criminals. Keep your stuff safe at all times, preferably in a crossbody bag or money belt, and avoid showing off valuables like costly jewellery or devices in public.

Use Licenced Transportation: When utilising taxis or ridesharing services, be sure you use licenced and recognised providers. Avoid hailing cabs from unmarked vehicles, and be wary of drivers who may attempt to overcharge or take needless diversions.

Be aware of traffic: Marseille's streets may be congested and chaotic, particularly during peak hours. When crossing the street, use caution and obey traffic lights and pedestrian crossing signs. To prevent penalties or accidents when driving, become familiar with local traffic rules and parking requirements.

Respect Local Customs and Laws: To prevent offending people or getting into trouble, familiarise yourself with Marseille's local customs and laws. For example, when visiting holy locations, dress modestly, avoid public drunkenness, and refrain from engaging in unlawful activities like drug use or soliciting.

Remain Hydrated and Sun-Protected: Marseille has a Mediterranean environment with scorching summers, so remain hydrated and shield yourself from the sun's rays. Bring a refillable water bottle, wear sunscreen, a hat, and sunglasses, and seek shade during the warmest hours of the day.

Trust Your Instincts: If anything feels odd or unpleasant, follow your instincts and leave the situation. Whether it's a worrisome meeting with a stranger or a dimly lit alleyway, prioritise your safety and seek help if necessary.

Stay Informed: Keep up with local news and any safety recommendations or warnings issued by authorities. Stay in touch with your hotel, tour companies, or local connections for advice on safe spots to visit and potential hazards to avoid.

Emergency Numbers

Medical Emergencies (Ambulance/Paramedics): Dial 15.

If you or someone else needs immediate medical assistance due to illness or injury, dialling 15 will link you to emergency medical services. Trained paramedics will be deployed to your area for help.

Fire Department (Firefighters): Dial 18.

In the case of a fire or other fire-related emergency, phone 18 to contact the fire department. They will deploy firemen who are prepared to handle the issue quickly and effectively.

Police Assistance (Law Enforcement): dial 17.

If you witness a crime, are in danger or need police help for any reason, call 17. This will link you to the police emergency line. Law enforcement personnel will attend to your call and offer help as needed.

Tips for Travelers

Packing Essentials

Comfortable Clothing: Because Marseille has a Mediterranean environment, bring lightweight, breathable clothing appropriate for warm weather. Remember to pack suitable walking shoes for exploring the city's cobblestone streets and mountainous landscape.

Sun Protection: With so many sunny days, sunscreen, sunglasses, and a wide-brimmed hat are important for shielding oneself from the harsh Mediterranean sun.
Swimwear & Beach Gear: Marseille has beautiful beaches such as Plage du Prado and Calanque de Sormiou, so bring your swimwear, beach towel and other beach needs for a pleasant day by the sea.

Travel adaptor: Make sure you have the correct travel adaptor to charge your electrical equipment, as the plug outlets in Marseille may differ from those in your own country.

Stay hydrated while exploring the city by bringing a reusable water bottle. Marseille has various water fountains where you can fill your bottle with safe drinking water.

French Phrasebook or Language App: While many locals speak English, knowing a few basic French words will improve your experience and allow you to communicate with them.

A lightweight daypack or tote bag is ideal for transporting basics such as water, food, a camera, and souvenirs while seeing Marseille's sights.

Rain Gear: Although Marseille has a largely sunny environment, it's a good idea to bring a compact umbrella or a lightweight rain jacket for unexpected storms, especially if you're going during the shoulder seasons.

Prescriptions and First-Aid Kit: Include any prescription prescriptions you may require, as well as a basic first-aid kit with bandages, pain relievers, and antiseptic wipes.

Travel papers and Insurance: Remember to keep your passport, travel insurance information, and any other important travel papers in a safe and immediately accessible area.

Etiquette And Customs

Greetings: In Marseille, greetings play an essential role in social interactions. When meeting someone for the first time or entering a business or restaurant, it is courteous to greet them with a cheerful "Bonjour" (hello) or "Bonsoir" (good evening), depending on the time of day. Handshakes are customary in official settings, but friends and acquaintances might exchange kisses on the cheeks, beginning with the left. Respect for personal space: Although Marseille is recognised for its warmth and friendliness, it is critical to respect others' personal space. If you're not familiar with someone, avoid standing too near or touching them.

Dress code: Marseille is a multicultural city with a variety of cultures and lifestyles. While casual wear is normally appropriate, it is best to dress modestly while visiting religious places or high-end enterprises. Beachwear is appropriate on the beach, but not in other public locations.

Dining etiquette: When eating out, it is traditional to wait until everyone has been served before beginning to eat. Keep your hands on the table, wrists resting on the edge, and avoid putting your elbows on the table. It is customary to say "Bon appétit" before beginning your meal and "Merci" (thank you) to the waitress afterward.

Language: Although many Marseille residents speak English, French is the predominant language. Making an attempt to utter a few simple French words, such as "Bonjour" and "Merci," is welcomed and demonstrates respect for the local culture.

Tipping: Tipping is not required in Marseille because a service charge is typically included on the bill. However, a little gratuity for excellent service is much appreciated.

Cultural sensitivity: Marseille is a cultural melting pot with people from many different backgrounds. Be mindful of cultural differences and refrain from making assumptions or generalisations about someone based on their race or religion.

CONCLUSION

Top 10 Things To Do

Explore Vieux Port (Old Port): Begin your adventure in the heart of Marseille by wandering around the ancient Vieux Port. Watch fisherman unload their catch, visit attractive waterfront cafés, and enjoy the lively scene.

Visit Notre-Dame de la Garde: Located on a hill above the city, Notre-Dame de la Garde provides magnificent views of Marseille and its surrounding coastline. Explore this historic church, which is covered with colourful mosaics and boasts breathtaking architecture.

Explore Le Panier: Lose yourself in the twisting lanes of Marseille's oldest neighbourhood, Le Panier. Admire bright street art, visit boutique boutiques, and savour local cuisine at modest cafés nestled in this lovely neighbourhood.

Indulge in Marseille's culinary scene. Enjoy Marseille's gastronomic pleasures, including savoury bouillabaisse (traditional fish stew) and freshly baked pastries. Visit the city's bustling markets, such as Marché des Capucins, to try local vegetables and delicacies.

A boat excursion allows you to explore Marseille's gorgeous coastline and adjacent Calanques. Admire the craggy cliffs, crystal-clear waves, and secret coves of this breathtaking natural reserve.

Visit MuCEM and immerse yourself in Mediterranean culture and history. Explore intriguing exhibitions, meander through spectacular buildings, and take in panoramic views of the sea.

Wander around Le Corbusier's Cité Radieuse: Architecture fans should not miss the opportunity to explore Cité Radieuse, Le Corbusier's masterwork of modernist architecture. Take a guided tour of this landmark skyscraper and learn about its revolutionary design principles.

Relax at Plage du Prado: Enjoy Marseille's sandy beaches at Plage du Prado. This vast beach has something for everyone, whether you want to relax in the sun, go for a refreshing swim, or participate in water sports.

Hike in Calanques National Park: Put on your hiking boots and discover the stunning landscapes of Calanques National Park. Choose from a range of hiking paths that will take you through mountainous terrain, past blue waterways, and to breathtaking views.

Experience Marseille's Nightlife: As the sun goes down, immerse yourself in Marseille's dynamic nightlife scene. From fashionable pubs and live music venues to bustling nightclubs, there are plenty of alternatives to keep you dancing till the early hours.

3 Days Itinerary

Day 1: Discovering Marseille's Historic Charm

Morning:

Start your day with a visit to the iconic Vieux Port (Old Port), the heart of Marseille. Take in the bustling atmosphere, watch fishermen unload their catch, and admire the picturesque boats.

Enjoy a leisurely breakfast at one of the charming cafes lining the port, savoring freshly baked pastries and a cup of rich French coffee.

Afternoon:

Explore Le Panier, Marseille's oldest district, known for its narrow streets, colorful facades, and vibrant street art. Wander through its maze-like alleys, stopping to admire local boutiques, artisan workshops, and hidden gems.

Visit the historic Fort Saint-Jean, which offers panoramic views of the Mediterranean Sea and the city skyline. Explore its impressive architecture and learn about Marseille's maritime history at the adjacent Museum of European and Mediterranean Civilizations (MuCEM).

Evening:

Indulge in Marseille's culinary delights with dinner at a traditional Provençal restaurant. Sample regional specialties such as bouillabaisse (fish stew) or socca (chickpea pancake) paired with local wine.

Take a sunset stroll along the Corniche Kennedy, a scenic coastal road lined with palm trees and offering breathtaking views of the Mediterranean. Marvel at the changing colors of the sky as the sun dips below the horizon.

Day 2: Exploring Marseille's Cultural Treasures

Morning:

Begin your day with a visit to the Palais Longchamp, a magnificent 19th-century monument housing the Museum of Fine Arts and the Natural History Museum. Explore its grand architecture, lush gardens, and impressive collections of art and artifacts.

Afternoon:

Head to the vibrant neighborhood of Cours Julien, known for its bohemian atmosphere, street art, and eclectic cafes. Spend some time browsing the local shops, art galleries, and artisan markets.

Visit the Notre-Dame de la Garde basilica, Marseille's most iconic landmark, perched atop a hill overlooking the city. Marvel at its stunning Byzantine architecture and panoramic views of Marseille and the Mediterranean Sea.

Evening:

Enjoy dinner at a seafood restaurant along the Corniche Kennedy, savoring freshly caught fish and seafood dishes.

Experience Marseille's lively nightlife scene with a visit to Le Vieux Panier or La Plaine, two popular districts known for their bars, live music venues, and cultural events.

Day 3: Escaping to Nature and Relaxation

Morning:

Take a day trip to the Calanques National Park, a breathtaking natural reserve located just outside Marseille. Hike along scenic trails, swim in crystal-clear coves, and marvel at the rugged limestone cliffs and turquoise waters.

Afternoon:

Enjoy a leisurely picnic lunch overlooking the Calanques, surrounded by pristine nature and stunning coastal scenery.

Alternatively, spend the afternoon relaxing on one of Marseille's beautiful beaches, such as Plage des Catalans or Prado Beach. Take a refreshing dip in the Mediterranean Sea or simply soak up the sun on the golden sands.

Evening:

Return to Marseille and unwind with a sunset cruise along the coastline, admiring the city's landmarks from the water.

Conclude your day with a farewell dinner at a seaside restaurant, savoring the flavors of Provencal cuisine one last time before bidding Marseille adieu

7 Days Itinerary

Day 1: Arrival and Orientation

Arrive in Marseille and settle into your accommodation.

Take a leisurely stroll around the Vieux Port (Old Port), soaking in the bustling atmosphere and admiring the picturesque harbor.

Enjoy a traditional Marseille meal at one of the waterfront restaurants, savoring fresh seafood dishes like bouillabaisse.

Wander through Le Panier, the city's oldest neighborhood, with its charming narrow streets and vibrant street art.

Day 2: Explore Historic Sites

Begin your day with a visit to the majestic Notre-Dame de la Garde basilica, offering panoramic views of the city and the Mediterranean Sea.

Explore the historic Fort Saint-Jean and Fort Saint-Nicolas, which guard the entrance to the Old Port.

Discover Marseille's rich maritime history at the Museum of European and Mediterranean Civilisations (MuCEM).

End the day with a sunset walk along the Corniche Kennedy, enjoying the sea breeze and views of the coastline.

Day 3: Cultural Immersion

Dive into Marseille's cultural scene with a visit to Palais Longchamp, home to the city's fine arts museum and natural history museum.

Explore the vibrant street art of Cours Julien and La Plaine, where colorful murals adorn the walls.

Spend the afternoon browsing the shops and cafes of the trendy Le Cours Julien district.

In the evening, catch a performance at the historic Opéra de Marseille or a live music show at one of the city's many venues.

Day 4: Day Trip to Calanques National Park

Embark on a day trip to Calanques National Park, a stunning natural reserve of rugged limestone cliffs, turquoise waters, and hidden coves.

Hike one of the park's scenic trails, such as the renowned Calanque d'En-Vau, or opt for a boat tour to explore the calanques from the sea.

Enjoy a picnic lunch surrounded by breathtaking coastal scenery.

Return to Marseille in the evening and relax with a seafood dinner at one of the portside restaurants.

Day 5: Culinary Delights

Indulge in a culinary adventure with a guided food tour of Marseille's markets, sampling local specialties like socca (chickpea pancake) and pastis (anise-flavored liqueur).

Learn the secrets of Provençal cuisine with a cooking class led by a local chef, where you'll prepare traditional dishes using fresh, seasonal ingredients.

In the evening, dine at a Michelin-starred restaurant or opt for a more casual meal at a bistro showcasing modern Mediterranean cuisine.

Day 6: Outdoor Adventures

Start the day with a hike or bike ride in the Calanques National Park, exploring scenic trails and secluded beaches.

Head to the Frioul Islands, a short boat ride from Marseille, to snorkel in crystal-clear waters and explore historic sites like the Château d'If.

Return to the mainland and unwind with a leisurely stroll along the Vallon des Auffes, a picturesque fishing village tucked away along the coastline.

Enjoy a seafood dinner at one of the waterfront restaurants overlooking the Vallon des Auffes.

Day 7: Relaxation and Departure

Spend your final day in Marseille relaxing and soaking up the Mediterranean sun at one of the city's beaches, such as Plage des Catalans or Prado Beach.

Take a scenic drive along the Route des Crêtes, winding along the rugged coastline and offering breathtaking views of the sea and cliffs.

Reflect on your time in Marseille over a farewell dinner, savoring the flavors of Provence one last time before departing.

Advice For All Kinds of Travellers

First Time Travellers:

Become Directional: Before you come, familiarize yourself with the city's layout, important landmarks, and available transit.

Learn the fundamentals of French: Even though most people in the area understand English, being able to communicate in a few simple French words will greatly improve your encounter and foster a relationship.

Safety Awareness: Like any large city, Marseille may have less safe sections, especially after dark. Remain in areas with good lighting and pay attention to your surroundings.

Discover Old Port (Vieux Port): With its stunning views, lively markets, and plenty of food options, this historic port neighborhood is a perfect place for first-time tourists to start their exploration.

Sample the Cuisine of the Area: Savor the delectable seafood delicacies and the well-known bouillabaisse of Marseille. Explore outside of tourist destinations to find real restaurants that are loved by locals and tourist.

For Solo Travellers:

Connect with Locals: Take guided tours, attend local events, or utilize social media to meet other visitors or friendly locals who may offer insider information.

Stay in Social Accommodations: Consider hostels or boutique hotels with a social ambiance, where you may quickly meet other lone travelers.

Safety precautions: Maintain vigilance, especially while exploring strange territory alone. Avoid wandering alone at night and keep your valuables safe.

Take a Walking Tour: A guided walking tour is an excellent way to safely explore Marseille while learning about its history, culture, and hidden jewels.

Embrace Solo Dining: Do not be frightened to eat alone! Many Marseille restaurants provide outside seating or communal tables, allowing you to enjoy your lunch while people-watching.

For LGBTQ Tourists:

Explore LGBTQ-Friendly Areas: Marseille has a vibrant LGBTQ scene, especially in the Le Panier and Cours Julien neighborhoods, with many LGBTQ-friendly bars, cafes, and clubs.

Connect with the Local LGBTQ Community: Look for LGBTQ events, organizations, or social groups to meet locals and fellow travelers, as well as find LGBTQ-friendly venues and activities.

Stay in LGBT-Friendly Accommodations: Look for hotels or guesthouses that are LGBTQ travel organization members or advertise as LGBTQ-friendly.

Attend LGBTQ Events: Check out Marseille's LGBTQ events calendar for festivals, pride celebrations, or cultural events that cater to the LGBTQ community.

Respect Local Customs: While Marseille is generally LGBTQ-friendly, it's important to be aware of cultural differences and to show respect for local customs

Printed in Great Britain
by Amazon

42063700R00066